Honor Series | *Honoring*
First Lady Melania
Book 2

By Rebecca Lynn

Copyright © 2022 Rebecca Lynn
Graphic design by Kristine Nicoletti

All rights reserved. No part of this book may be reproduced or transmitted in any form or by any means, electronic or mechanical, including photocopy, recording, scanning, or by any information storage and retrieval system, without the written permission of the author, except where permitted by law.

All photographs "Courtesy of Donald J. Trump Presidential Library." Public Domain.

Published in the United States by Rebecca Lynn Books

Manufactured in the United States of America
First Printing ISBN: 978-1-951167-17-2

Dear First Lady Melania Trump,

You have done more for us than I ever realized.

Thank you.

Dear Children,

Before we begin, let's talk about what it means to honor our First Lady Melania.

We honor First Lady Melania when we learn what she has done for our country. Then we honor her by being thankful for all she has done. A thankful heart is a heart that honors.

Speaking truth about someone is a way to show honor. When you tell others the truth you learn about First Lady Melania and the many amazing things she has done for us, you are showing honor to her. This is a wonderful thing to do.

Another way to honor First Lady Melania is to thank Jesus for her and pray for her. First Lady Melania is honored by your prayers!

One more thing for you to know. You are honoring First Lady Melania just by reading the pages of this book. You are off to a great start in honoring her. Well done!

First Lady Melania is loving.

First Lady Melania has a very loving heart. You can tell this by how she treats people. First Lady Melania treats both adults and children with kindness, compassion, and goodness. She knows that when people are treated this way they feel loved, and everyone wants to feel loved. First Lady Melania teaches us that to love others is a beautiful thing.

Let's honor First Lady Melania for being loving.

First Lady Melania is classy.

First Lady Melania dresses with grace and style. She always wears beautiful clothes. But that isn't what makes her classy. She's classy because she shows respect to all the people who serve her and her husband. She carries her head high and helps others to do the same. The people who protect her love doing so, because she treats them very well. This is what it means to be classy.

Let's honor First Lady Melania for being classy.

First Lady Melania is intelligent.

First Lady Melania uses her intelligence to bless people. We should do this too. She used her intelligence to create her BE BEST program. One of the things BE BEST does is teach children the importance of their emotional, social, and physical health. When children are healthy they can thrive.

Also, did you know that First Lady Melania speaks several languages? She does! This is an intelligent and amazing thing that very few people in the world can do.

Let's honor First Lady Melania for being intelligent.

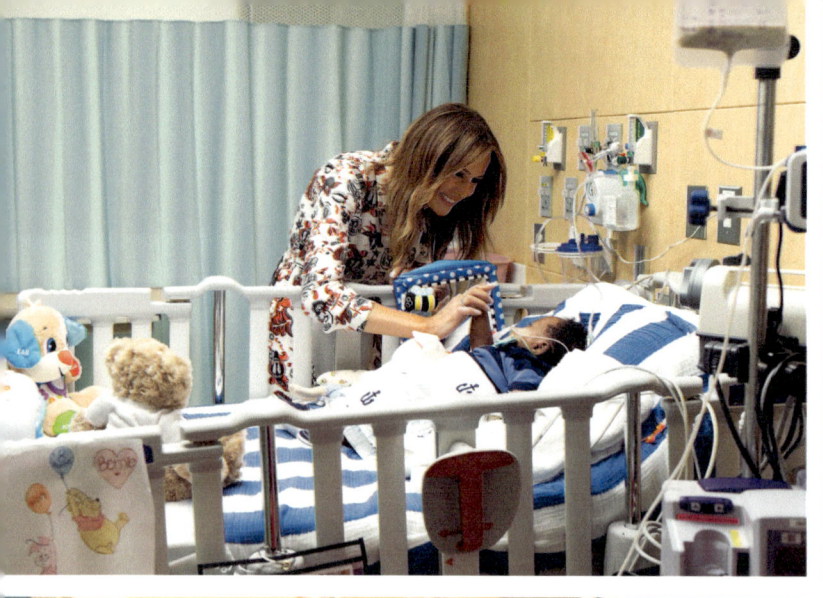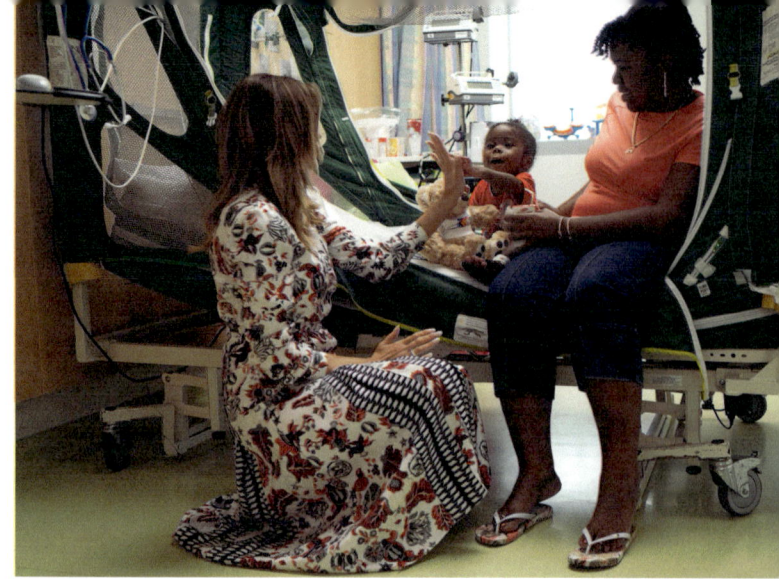

First Lady Melania is caring.

First Lady Melania cares deeply for children and wants all children to know this. One way she showed her care is by visiting children in the hospital. She gave much love and compassion in doing so. This blessed not only the children, but their parents as well. Expressing care to others can help them get better. This is a wonderful thing to do.

Let's honor
First Lady Melania for being caring.

First Lady Melania is supportive.

First Lady Melania supports our military. Our military work hard to keep America safe and free. First Lady Melania has shown her support by visiting them when she is able. In this way, she also shows her concern, care, and gratitude to them. She is proud of the work they do. You can tell this makes them very happy!

Let's honor
First Lady Melania for being supportive.

34 109
MARGARET A
HIS WIFE
JUN 11 1921
DEC 10 2003
U.S.ARMY
U.S.ARMY
34 110
KATHRYN
HIS WIFE
SEP 27 1924
NOV 27 1997
34 285

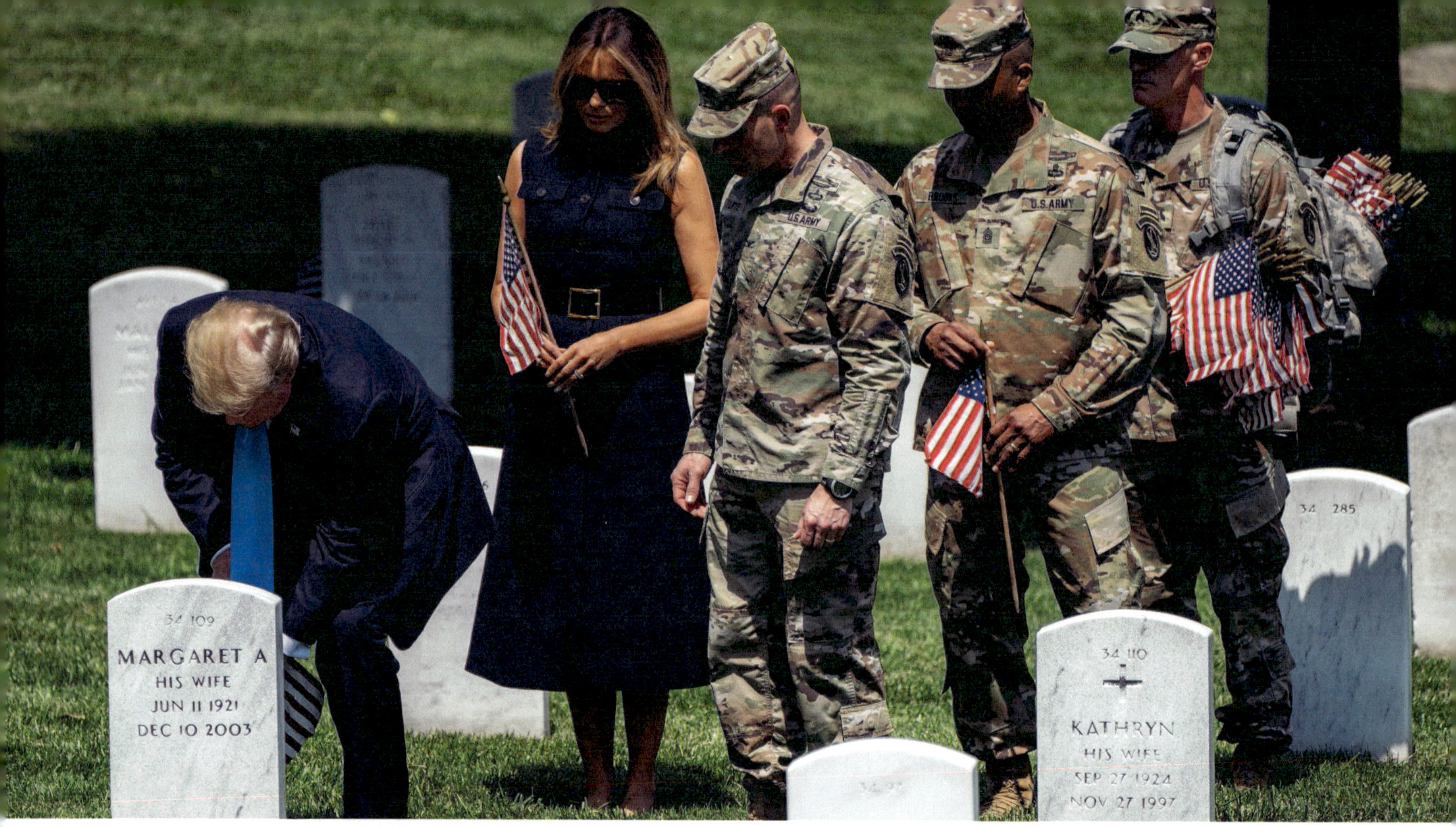

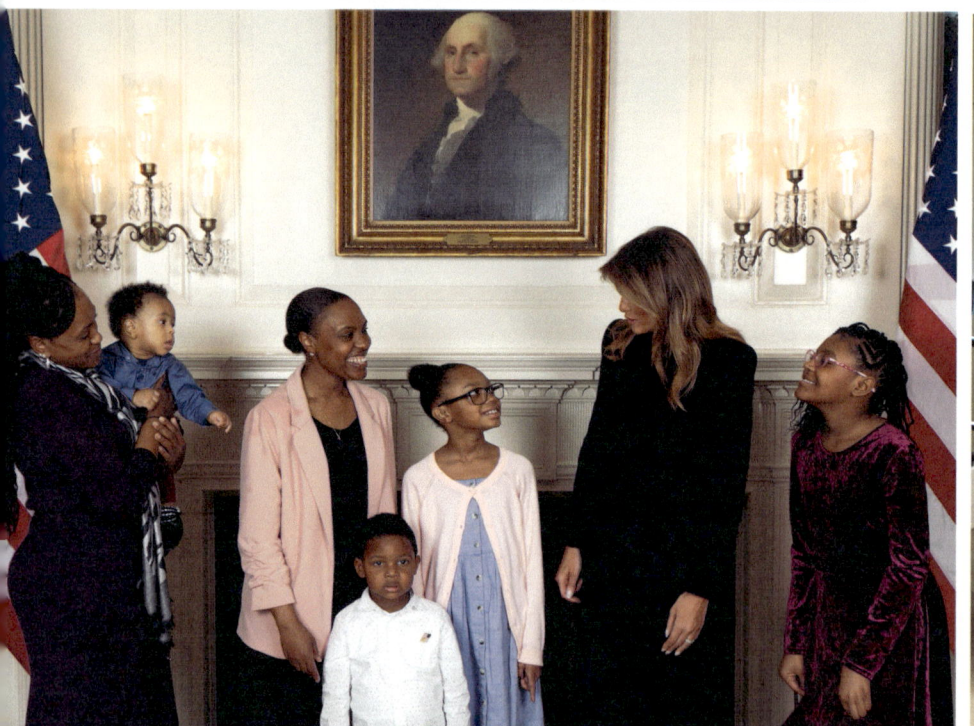

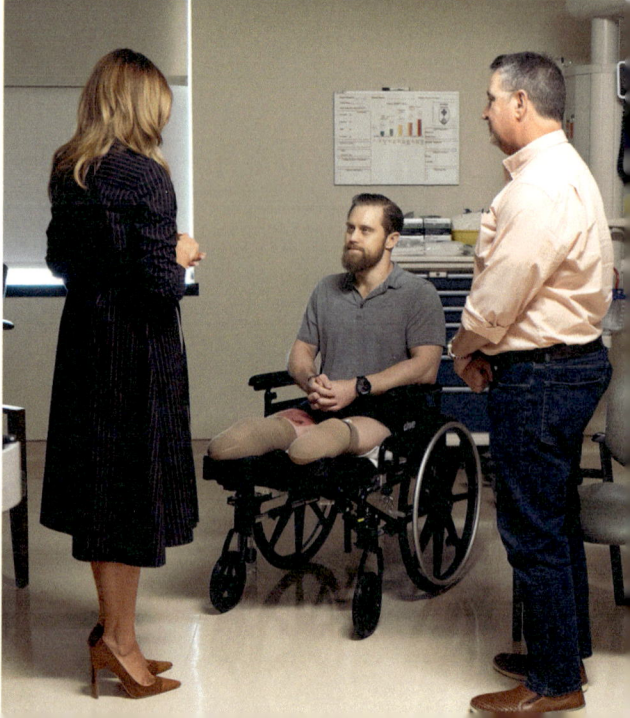

First Lady Melania is emotionally strong.

First Lady Melania is an emotionally strong person. Someone who is emotionally strong can use their emotions to support, bless, and encourage others. They can laugh with people who laugh and cry with people who cry. They can be with people who are hurting, even when it is hard to do so. First Lady Melania does this. She has helped many people by being emotionally strong for them.

Let's honor First Lady Melania for being emotionally strong.

First Lady Melania is thankful.

First Lady Melania is a thankful person. Can you tell who she is thanking in these pictures? If you said "God," you are right! First Lady Melania has shared many times that she is thankful to God for all He has done. We should all be thankful to God too. He saves us and blesses us in so many ways.

Let's honor First Lady Melania for being thankful.

BE BEST
adidas

BE BEST

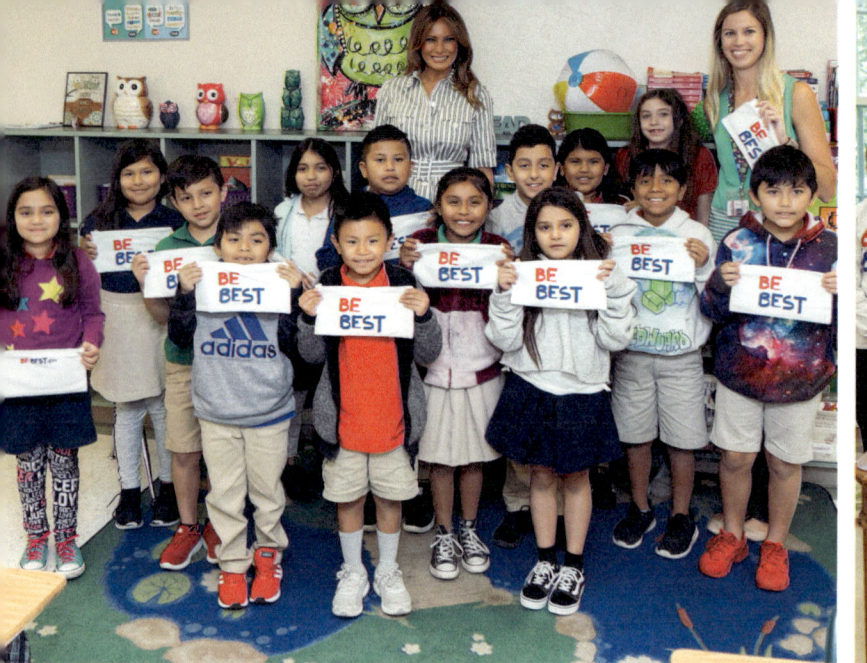

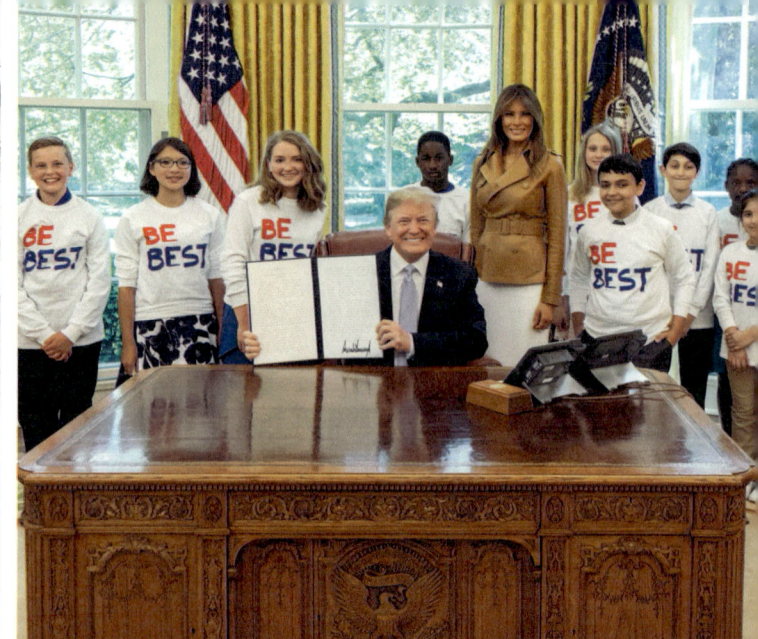

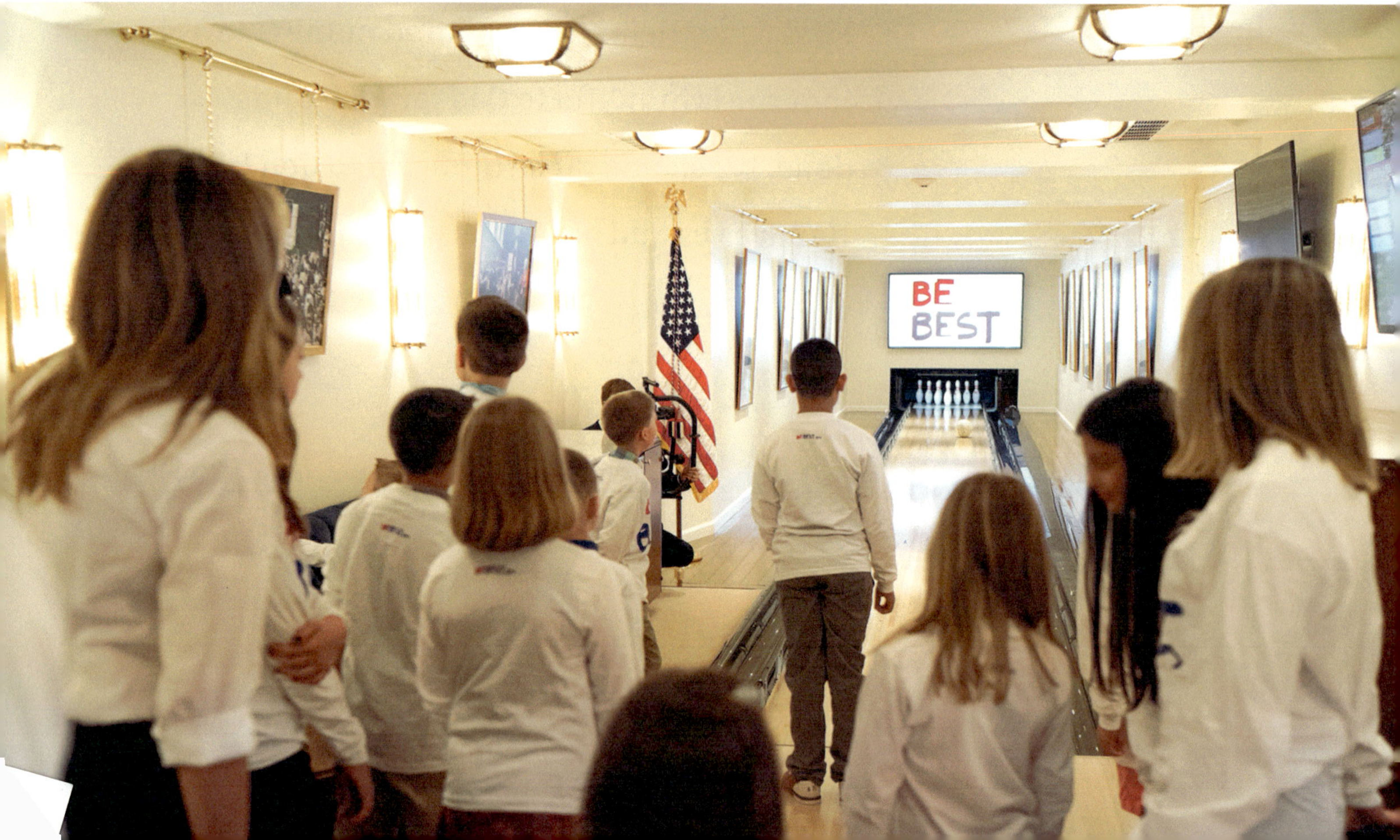
BE BEST

First Lady Melania is a woman who dreams big.

First Lady Melania has shown us she is a woman who dreams big and is willing to put much effort into making her dreams come true. Her dreams have blessed many, many children. Her BE BEST program teaches children they have value and worth and that their health and safety are very important. We can all follow First Lady Melania's example to dream big dreams and know that our dreams can bless others too!

Let's honor First Lady Melania for dreaming big dreams.

First Lady Melania is courageous.

First Lady Melania is a woman of courage. She knew that when her husband became President, bad people would want to harm her and her family. She didn't let this stop her though. Instead, she used her courage to focus on helping others rather than being afraid. Her BE BEST program helps children in America and all over the world. We should use our courage to help others too.

Let's honor First Lady Melania for being courageous.

First Lady Melania honors others.

First Lady Melania is an honorable person and shows honor to others. She often honors her husband (our President) by speaking positively about him. She shares the wonderful things she loves about him and praises him for his hard work. God is honored when wives honor their husbands this way.

Let's honor First Lady Melania for honoring others.

First Lady Melania is concerned.

First Lady Melania wore this dress to a special event. What do you see when you look at it? This dress shows drawings from little children who needed help. Our President and First Lady worked with the military and other trained adults to give these children the help they needed. First Lady Melania wore this dress to show America she is concerned about these children, and that something was being done to help them. Many people were grateful to see this, as they were concerned too.

Let's honor First Lady Melania for being concerned.

Are you getting a glimpse as to why we should honor First Lady Melania?

Here are some more things to know about her.

First Lady Melania loves children.

So many pictures show us how much First Lady Melania loves children. First Lady Melania has visited children all over America and all around the world. She has gone to hospitals and schools to be with children, and she's hosted fun events for children to come too. She wants children to know they are important and lovable.

Let's honor
First Lady Melania for loving children.

First Lady Melania loves our country.

First Lady Melania has shown how much she loves our country by how hard she has worked for us. Look back through the pictures of this book. They show us some of the lives she has touched, the hard work she has done, and effort she has given. She has served America well and done more for us than we know. We should all be very grateful for her.

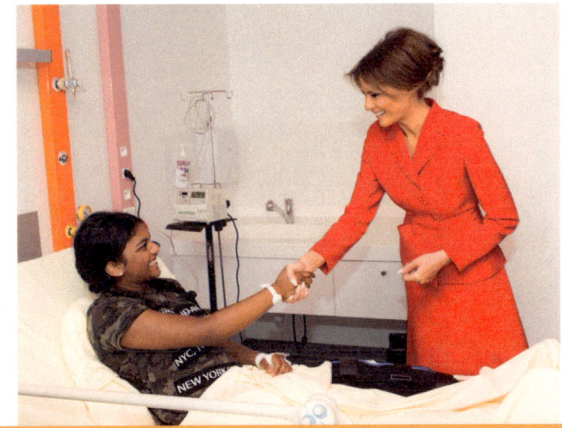

Let's honor
First Lady Melania for loving our country.

First Lady Melania loves God.

First Lady Melania talks often about the goodness of God and how thankful she is to Him. She has shared prayers on social media for all of us to read. She gives glory to God for all He has done for all people.

Let's honor First Lady Melania for loving God.

Dear Parents,

The media lied to us. We should have been able to trust them, but they were not trustworthy. They lied to us about many things, but especially about President Trump and First Lady Melania. Not only did they lie, but they also hid the truth.

I hope what you have learned encourages you to learn more. The truth is out there; you just have to search to find it. President Trump and First Lady Melania have done so many amazing things for America and for the world. I could only list a few. They really are wonderful people, who deeply love our country and paid a price to serve us. I hope you will look and find out more about them.

Pray for discernment as you research, and pray for God to lead you to the truth. He will. God wants us to know the truth, for it is the truth that sets us free.

I pray God's richest blessings over you, your family, and our great country, America. The best really is to come!!

More Books by Rebecca Lynn

Baby Board Books

coming soon!

Children's Books

coming soon!   coming soon!   coming soon!

Made in United States
Troutdale, OR
01/22/2025

28256357R00026